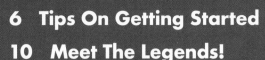

**PLUS!
PUZZLES &
ANSWERS
22, 54
& 92**

INSIDE

11 SQUA

10 QUICK TIPS
FOR GETTING STARTED

In the world of Apex Legends, the key to getting ahead is teamwork!

As a beginner, Apex Legends can be pretty daunting. After all, it seems like everyone else has been playing the game for months and had more than enough time to hone their skills.

But that doesn't mean you can't catch up! Here are 10 quick tips and tricks to help kickstart your Apex Legends career.

1 Choose a character that suits you

Choosing the right character can be difficult if you've never played a game like Apex Legends before. If you're not used to Battle Royales or team games, how do you play video games in general? If you're an aggressive, in the face, no holds barred sort of player, an offensive character like Bangalore or Wraith would work well for you. But if you prefer to provide defence or health to your team, Gibraltar or Lifeline would be a good choice. Once you figure out your playstyle, choosing a character becomes much simpler.

Currently, there are nine Legends to choose from

2
Stick with your team!

Apex Legends is played in a team of three, and nothing riles people more than someone who isn't a team player. Of course, some characters work best at a respectful distance, but that doesn't mean you should be flying solo. When you and your team first launch, there's an option to divert paths and fly away. Doing so at a short distance is fine, but going off alone often leads to dying early or resentment from your team.

3
Use the Ping system as much as possible

The Ping system is revolutionary in a lot of ways, but most importantly it lets you communicate with your team without using your voice. You can Ping the way you want your squad to go, if you see an enemy and want to warn everyone, and even if you see some equipment you know will benefit your team. And as it's so fast, you can communicate in half the time it takes to speak.

It may not be the best gear, but it's a start!

4
Don't quit after you die

What makes Apex Legends a unique Battle Royale game is that once you die, you get the opportunity to come back and kick ass. What's more, you can respawn as many times as you want, as long as there's someone else alive in your team. All they need to do is come and recover your death box, then respawn you once they get to a checkpoint.

5
Loot everything!

Depending on where you drop, you could find yourself with a lot of great or terrible loot. Regardless, pick up everything you see. Whether you're playing with friends or not, it's first come, first served. Grab everything – grenades, shotgun bolts you don't need just yet... Something is better than nothing, especially to take on enemies who drop in the same spot as you.

6 Punch!

Punching in Apex Legends is much more effective than it looks. If you land in the same zone as the enemy, but find yourself without a gun, you can effectively punch the enemy to knock them off balance, making you harder to hit. This isn't an end-all solution, of course, so only use it when your options are limited.

Punching is your best weapon when you have no weapon

7 Be aware of your surroundings

As a beginner, you can't expect to know the map, but be aware of the area around you. Are you in a building with only one way in and out? That can be effective as an ambush, but also lead to you being trapped. Are you out in the open? If you are, you can be spotted by other players, particularly enemy snipers. Look for places where you can hide or move behind. Just be careful, as you never know who's out there watching!

8 Upgrade your gear!

So you've snagged two weapons and a body shield. Great, but you can always do better. As you continue gunning and running, you'll come across different attachments that upgrade your guns. A fully upgraded weapon is better than one with no upgrades at all, so be sure to pick up these parts whenever you stumble on them.

ALTERNATOR SMG

OWNED 2/40

Warm Rave

The Alternative Remedy

Search & Rescue

LED Rez

The Galvanizer

Eye of the Storm

Trial by Fire

Code of Honor

Off the Grid

Break the Enemy

Out for Blood

Back

Gun down stragglers as they come out of the circle!

9 Check your map to see where the next Ring is

The Ring in Apex Legends is the area of safety where you can move without taking damage. Some players aren't too bothered about the circle, but that soon becomes their downfall as their health slowly starts to drain away. Opening the map and checking where the next Ring is can save you a lot of trouble. For one thing, it can help you plan where to go next, and you can also wait for stragglers coming out of the circle and gun them down!

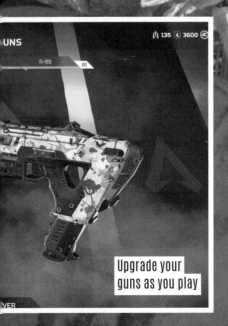

Upgrade your guns as you play

10 Don't be afraid to try new things!

We're not saying 'look at the rest of the nine tips and throw them out of the window,' but being creative can often bag you a win. Sticking to the tried and true path is great, but sometimes you'll be forced to think on the spot and be unique in how you handle the situation. But don't fear that – it just means you're one step closer to becoming a fully fledged Apex legend!

KNOW THE LEGENDS

Here's our guide to the original characters of Apex Legends...

Bangalore

Bangalore is great for new players and those unfamiliar with the Battle Royale genre. She can deal a lot of damage, and has abilities that can help disengage when things get really hairy. All in all, Bangalore is fairly well balanced, but even she has weaknesses and strengths that the player can exploit for their own benefit. Such as...

to confuse the enemy team and send them crying back to where they came from? Chuck that grenade and get shooting!

■ Bangalore's passive ability, Double Time, lets you sprint faster while being shot at. This makes Bangalore much easier to manoeuvre into cover or off a cliff to safety.

STRENGTHS:

■ Bangalore's smoke grenade ability allows her to both hide and get the drop on someone in a fight. Want to revive a teammate? Pop the smoke grenade and administer that medical care! Want

WEAKNESSES:

■ Bangalore's ultimate, Rolling Thunder, isn't very useful. While it can target enemies, calling it in takes a while, and in that time the enemy could have gotten away or shot you in the face.

Caustic

Caustic isn't the worst character in the world to play, but he most certainly isn't the best. In fact, like Gibraltar, he's a moving target, particularly out in the open. Even a person with a pretty terrible aim can hit Caustic out in the field. But like every Legend, there's some good with the bad.

STRENGTHS:

■ Caustic is a king at close combat. He has six gas canisters that he can place behind doors, which will easily gas you the moment you're in the room. With this, he'll dominate combat and you'll wonder why you ever bothered going face to face with him in such close quarters.
■ Caustic works well with Mirage's decoys if you want to bait people into coming your way. They'll see the Mirage, get all trigger happy and fall right into your trap. He also works with Bloodhound's ultimate ability to allow your team to see enemies through your gas.

WEAKNESSES:

■ Like Gibraltar, Caustic has a huge hitbox. Unlike Gibraltar, he hasn't got any defensive abilities that could soak up that damage. If you're out in the open as Caustic, you better start running as fast as you can!
■ Caustic's abilities aren't the best and fully fledged only really work in tight-knit quarters. In fact, throwing his ultimate – aka the gas bomb – out into the open is useless, as it's easy to run out of it and into clearer air.

CAUSTIC
Toxic Trapper

BLOODHOUND / GIBRALTAR / LIFELINE / PATHFINDER / OCTANE

WRAITH / BANGALORE / CAUSTIC / MIRAGE

Caustic may look cool but has some serious drawbacks

Bangalore is the best choice for new players

11

Octane

The newest Legend is anything but slow, but what about his abilities outside of speed? Well, it's a little complicated...

STRENGTHS:

■ Octane can run circles around his enemies, thanks to his Adrenaline Junkie ability. It's difficult to land a hit on him.

■ His ultimate, Launch Pad, is very useful for escaping some prickly situations. It can also be used to enter a firefight, surprising your enemies with your sudden appearance.

■ Octane can heal over time, thanks to his passive ability, making him one of only two characters that can do some sort of healing in the game, even if it's just to himself.

WEAKNESSES:

■ Octane doesn't have the best abilities when it comes to combat. While he can move himself and his team around fast with his Jump Pad, he has no abilities to help you fight enemies better.

■ Using his ability Adrenaline Junkie whilst in battle will get you killed very quickly if you're not careful.

> **Octane can easily run circles around his enemies**

Octane is for those who like to be quick on their feet

Gibraltar

Gibraltar is a giant of a man and one of the few Legends who just wants to make the world a better place. However, while his abilities aren't all that bad, he suffers from a huge hitbox and, like Bangalore, an ultimate that's only sometimes useful.

STRENGTHS:

■ Gibraltar's Dome of Protection ability is great for covering your back when escaping from the enemy, reviving someone or if you want to bait your enemy into

Bloodhound

Bloodhound is a powerful character in the right hands. They have extraordinary tracking abilities and can easily lead their team to victory. However, they're not a meat shield, so shouldn't be left to soak up the damage while you think up strategies.

Bloodhound is an incredible tracker

STRENGTHS:

■ Bloodhound's ultimate, Beast of the Hunt, is great for allowing you to see the outline of enemies, so you can rush up and take them out unawares.

■ Their Eye of the All-Father ability is great for revealing traps, clues and enemies, effectively making you the perfect player to scout ahead.

WEAKNESSES:

■ Bloodhound has no abilities that will help you get out of combat in a hurry.

■ They're more suited to scouting and tracking than a full-blown shoot-up.

the Ring and settle this fight like true Apex Legends.

■ His passive, Gun Shield, is great for adding further protection to Gibraltar as you fight.

WEAKNESSES:

■ His hitbox is very big; if you're out in the open, you're going to get hit – a lot.

■ Gibraltar's ultimate is hard to time right, and enemies can get

Gibraltar is a force to be reckoned with, if played right

Wraith

Wraith is a powerful hero that some players may find intimidating to play as her abilities are hard to use effectively. While Bangalore may be easy to pick up, Wraith is the opposite, but that makes an expert Wraith player quite the opponent.

WRAITH
Interdimensional Skirmisher

Wraith will keep everyone on their toes

STRENGTHS:

■ Her Into the Void ability is great for escaping perilous situations, as well as sneaking around your enemies to shoot them in the back while your team distracts them.

■ She's a fast, sneaky character whose abilities help her move at a speed beaten only by Octane.

WEAKNESSES:

■ Wraith's Dimensional Rift can be easily exploited by the enemy, either by following her through the rift or waiting for her to appear on the other end.

■ Wraith's passive ability, Voices of the Void, isn't reliable. Too often, you'll get shot, then the voices will warn you.

Mirage

Mirage is a trickster, making him one of the more difficult Legends to battle against. You may think you're shooting at him, but in reality you're shooting one of his clones. But that doesn't mean he can't be taken down.

STRENGTHS:

■ Mirage's abilities can easily confuse his enemies, so he can make his move of attack, reposition himself or even escape.

■ His ultimate ability, Vanishing Act, is perfect for cloaking Mirage, but can also provide covering fire, as the clones will start to shoot at you the nearer you get.

WEAKNESSES:

■ Mirage is a bit of a one-trick pony. As you play more against him, you'll discover his clones are easy to tell apart and, if there are a tonne of Mirages, the real one will be nearby. Once that's figured out, Mirage can be easy to take down.

Mirage is a trickster, but he's not hard to figure out

Lifeline

Lifeline is the only Legend that can heal not just herself but the whole team with her Healing Drone. Without Lifeline, you'll need to rely on med-kits. Yet, while she is a valuable member of your team, she does have some weaknesses.

STRENGTHS:

- Lifeline's ultimate ability, Care Package, can give you the extra equipment you need. Purple armour, blue knockdown shields and the like. All of that's possible.
- Lifeline revives teammates much faster than the other Legends, and in doing so gets a shield to protect her as she brings you back to life.

WEAKNESSES:

- Lifeline's Care Package is useful, but it can also signal to enemies that you're nearby, effectively putting a huge X on you and your team.

L1   PLAY   BATTLE PASS   STORE   R1   135   4800   100

OCTANE

MIRAGE

Play Lifeline if you want healing frequently

15

APEX LEGENDS:
UNDERSTANDING THE MAP

Separate the beginner from the expert with these map tips

Apex Legends' map, Kings Canyon, is currently the only playable map, but we suspect that will change at some point in the near future. There are 17 named locations, all with varying opportunities of spawning low- to high-tier loot, plus some unnamed locations that also have their own share of goodies. So, depending on where you land, you'll either be able to grab some super-rare equipment or just pick up the minimum to survive.

Unfortunately, there's no guarantee where you can find the high-tier loot, but there are locations (listed opposite) where it's considered more likely.

High Tier

- Artillery
- Relay
- Runoff
- The Pit
- Airbase
- Bunker
- Swamps
- Thunderdome
- Repulsor
- Water Treatment

Mid-Tier

- Slum Lakes
- Cascades
- Wetlands
- Bridges
- Skull Town

Low Tier

- Hydro Dam
- Market

These locations all have different coloured tiers, which appear on the top-left corner of your screen, so you know what calibre of loot to expect when you get there. The highest tier is purple, the mid-tier is blue, and the lowest tier is white.

Hot Zones

Hot Zones appear on the map as pale blue circles and highlight areas where you'll see an increase in both the quality and quantity of loot, plus the chance of finding fully kitted weapons. These are highly desirable, as they come with all their possible attachments already equipped. Hot Zones can usually be spotted by bringing up the map, or as a strip of blue light while you're waiting to jump into battle. The problem is that you won't be the only ones heading in their direction, as they're pretty hard to miss. Often, you'll be forced to shoot your way out or run away, and escaping can be a lot harder than it looks.

Kings Canyon Map

20 SQUADS LEFT

SLUM LAKES
ARTILLERY
THE PIT
RED
RUNOFF
CASCADES
WETLANDS
BUNKER
AIRBASE
BRIDGES
SWAMPS
HYDRO DAM
MARKET
SKULL TOWN
REPULSOR
WATER TREATMENT

WAYPOINT   L2 / R2 ZOOM   REMOVE WAYPOINT

MAP FEATURES

Respawn Beacon
Bring banner to revive dead squad members.

Supply Ship
High tier loot barge.

Hot Zone
High tier loot zone. Chance for a fully kitted weapon.

Supply Drop
Chance for high tier loot.

Hot Zones appear on the map as pale blue circles

Supply Ships and Drops

As well as Hot Zones, you'll notice huge Supply Ships slowly moving across the map. Again, you'll likely spot one before you even drop down. They contain a stash of first-rate loot scattered over two floors. You can drop straight on to a ship at the beginning of a match, but as subsequent Supply Ships appear later on, it might be worth waiting and avoiding an early fight.

Supply Drops also feature on the map as small pulsing circles, and can often be seen or heard if you're close to one dropping. Similar to Lifeline's Care Package drops, they're red and only open manually. If you're not careful, you can easily pass one by, missing out on a pile of sweet, sweet loot. Don't be that person.

> **Supply Ships contain a stash of loot scattered over two floors**

Other important map features

LOOT TICKS These little robots carry high-tier loot and are colour-coded according to what they hide inside. Punching them or breaking them open with bullets will give you access to their goodies. They often make whirring noises, so listen carefully and you're sure to find one hidden away in a corner.

Loot Ticks are hidden across the map

Water Treatment is a good place to find high-tier loot

ZIP LINES If you're not playing Pathfinder, with his ziplines that move him and his team around the map at speed, your transport may be limited. Thankfully, several ziplines run both horizontally and vertically across the map to get you and your team moving quickly. You can jump off them at any time, so you're able to escape enemy fire if needed.

Zipline heaven!

ZIPLINE BALLOONS When you jump out of the dropship, you'll notice several red balloons in the sky. These are attached to ziplines, and if you interact with one it will fire you up into the air, then shoot you off in the direction of your choice. They're particularly useful if you're desperate to get out of the Ring before it catches up with you.

RESPAWN BEACONS Respawn Beacons allow you to bring your teammates back from the dead. They're scattered across the map, and can usually only be used once before becoming defunct.

WALLS AND CLIFFS Apex Legends' climbing mechanics are incredibly useful, whether you're peering over the edge of a cliff and watching for oncoming enemies, or vaulting over walls and making your escape. You'll come across a number of different walls and cliffs that you can climb on the map.

SUPPLY BINS These red and white cylinders are scattered all over the map. They can be a bit hit and miss when it comes to the quality of loot inside, as some contain fantastic gear and others are filled with duff items. Nonetheless, they're extremely useful and you should always check them out if they're closed.

WHERE DO I LAND?

The battle begins, but where should you start?

The first big decision you have to make in a match of Apex Legends is where to start. As you rocket down to Kings Canyon, where do you land? Which bit of the map is best to aim for?

First and foremost, it pays to land where you can quickly get hold of some good-quality loot. Even though the game doesn't tend to punish you for not kitting up quickly – and there are fewer players on the map than in most Battle Royale games – you still run the risk of being an easy kill if you leave it too long before arming yourself. That said, you won't be the only one with the same idea...

Peak areas

At the start of each skirmish, the game earmarks where to find the best loot. Look at the map as you enter the arena, and you'll see a big blue circle. The chances of finding something good in this Hot Zone are much stronger. We'll be talking about that Hot Zone quite a bit over the course of this book.

As well as that, though, the Supply Ship that appears at the beginning of each round is loaded with quality goodies, if you want to get the match off to a quick start. The downside? Well, you're going to run into trouble, and fast. Both the Hot Zone and Supply Ship attract good players pretty much instantly. You can expect the first firefights in a round to take place here, so make sure to keep your wits about you.

Thunderdome is quieter location

The fringes of the map are less busy

20 SQUADS LEFT

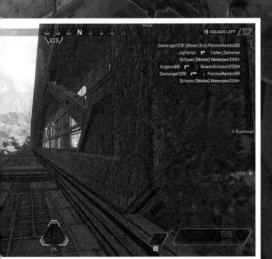

Hot Zones attract good players instantly

Quieter areas

If you like to take your time or aren't too experienced, head to some of the quieter parts of the map to get your initial loot together. The outskirts tend to be less busy. Head to any named location and you're bound to find some useful stuff, but the further you go from the centre the less likely you are to run into initial traffic. On the south side of the map, for instance, both Thunderdome and Water Treatment are generally solid locations for some quality pickups, and not too many other players initially venture there. Obviously, you'll need to keep an eye on the Ring closing in, and if you're on the fringes of the map you may have to cover a lot of ground quickly to get to safety! Remember that the map will continue to evolve and change over time, so some of the named locations may disappear and new ones will be added. That said, the more isolated an area is, the less likely it is to attract players.

EVOLUTION

More maps are very likely to be added to Apex Legends over time, but the guiding ideas will remain the same: stick to the fringes if you want quieter locations to build up your loot whilst avoiding other players.

PUZZLE PAGES

Test you brain with these teasers

WORDSEARCH

Can you hunt down the 25 Legends, weapons, places and Items from the grid? Good luck!

```
Q N D G Z B E P E U I H W S C H E H R O K
A K U T M A S T I F F D N C C I T S U A C
G U X M G T K F N L D P C W B S E G E X A
N F R I I T U S E I B S I I Z W O M J Y P
G I B R A L T A R F T H T N Q W S E U D X
A R P A F E J O O E U X E G M C R I L N E
O S R G S P F Z J L U B E M M L C A T F P
X T D E X A Q Y K I L H G A L U W P I T A
L U H M Q S H Q O N Z C U N X O E U M T S
R R V X U S W Q U E K M L S U O K E A Z H
Y B Z A S B R G M B N S B A B M I A T F I
G O G N O I U E B L O O D H O U N D E L E
F C F H O A D N P V G O Z T N I G U A V L
F H L A N C S J P E Y Z N T O N S Y C T D
B A C Z H B E W P W E H I Y O K C E C Y B
K R A B E R Q U S S I K P C L H A X E Q A
R G Z W H E Z T Q E X O E H M O N L L H T
X E I A W D C V W I D M O C H J Y D L Z T
U R M Y U N F I N K B A N G A L O R E O E
N A D W E I G E M K R M D V H E N G R Z R
Q A N H H F O G O O C T A N E N P G A P Y
C E O G J H Y N Z T S W J Z O G N T N J E
O B Q Y P T G L B H O K U C O F P I T V O
Y S U L W A R T I L L E R Y N M U N Z R C
Q E D Q D P O Z V R E I T N O R F D L I W
```

Apex Pack
Artillery
Bangalore
Battle Pass
Bloodhound
Caustic
Gibraltar
Hemlok
Hot Zone
Kings Canyon
Kraber
Lifeline
Mastiff
Mirage
Mozambique
Octane
Pathfinder
Peacekeeper
Phoenix Kit
Shield Battery
Turbocharger
Ultimate Accelerant
Wild Frontier
Wingman
Wraith

VIS-QUIZ

A keen eye is vital to success in Apex Legends, so sharpen up your acuity by working out which of the four patterns on the right is created by combining the two shapes on the left.

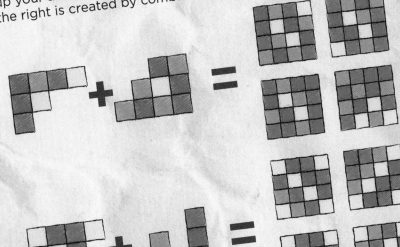

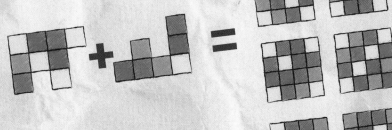

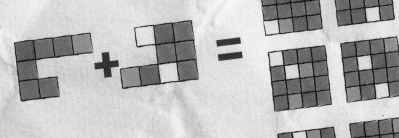

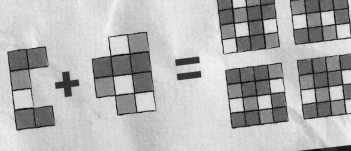

All the answers for these puzzles can be found on page 92. No cheating, though!

Mastering Apex Legends' non-verbal communication is a must if you want to win

GET PINGING!

Apex Legends became a quick phenomenon following its release at the start of 2019, and one of its key differentiators is its reliance on teamwork. The game goes to great lengths to promote mic-free communication. Read on to find out how to get the most out of its Ping system!

What's Pinging?

The Ping system is a context-specific command linked to a single button press. The premise is simple: aiming at an object, area or item and hitting RB (Xbox One) or R1 (PlayStation 4), or the middle mouse button (PC) will Ping

The top-right corner keeps track of any Pings, so keep an eye out

You - Suggested a location.
You - Pinged a location.
You - Canceled ping.

X Revive DUMMIE

CANCEL RB
GO 102m

15 30 NE 60 75 E 105 120

The Ping system can be used at any point in a match

your intentions to your teammates. This info is transferred by dialogue from one character to another, bringing more personality to each match.

While the Ping system may be a simple mechanic, its use can't be understated. It can be used at any point in a match. Before your team have launched from the dropship at the beginning of a round, you can Ping to suggest a location for the designated Jumpmaster to aim for. Likewise, the Jumpmaster themselves can Ping an area, and teammates can confirm or ignore this as they see fit. This simple interaction, combined with teams jumping together by default, prevents a match from becoming a trudge across a huge expanse to find your cohorts.

Once you're on the ground, Pinging becomes even more important. As you and your team split

off into individual buildings and begin scavenging for weapons and equipment, you'll likely locate items that are of no use to you or don't suit your playstyle. In this case, Ping it for your squad mates to find – you'll stand a much better chance if you're all equipped with decent equipment come the business end of a match.

Similarly, keep an eye (and ear) out for your squad's Pings. If they locate something ideal for your skillset or simply something that will give you a competitive advantage, you'll be able to claim "dibs" on the item using the Ping button. While there's always a chance a teammate will hoover up the item before you have the chance to, it does seem most will honour the dibs.

CANCEL

APEX APEX

Tell your squadmates where the loot is!

X Take Frag Grenade
X Take Thermite Grenade
Take Health

PING

PopPunkPanda

Keep an eye (and ear) out for your squad's Pings

Direction

You've landed, you've looted, and the Ring has begun to close. It's time to get moving, but in which direction? The Ping system is ideal for formulating a strategy through non-verbal communication, so why not suggest somewhere for teammates to move to? Just Ping a general direction to suggest it, or do it directly from the map screen. They can confirm with their own Ping (in the same way they did when initially jumping to the map), and it can be used to highlight key pieces of level geometry too. Ziplines, redeployment balloons and respawn areas can all be identified with your Ping.

This lets players organise themselves, but it's harder to do when the bullets are flying. While Pinging an escape route can be helpful, if you're looking to fight, there is a shortcut – if you double-tap the Ping button, you can instantly send an "enemy located" command. Pinging the enemy themselves also works, but with Apex Legends' impressive movement systems it can be difficult to line up your crosshairs for anything other than a shot.

Double-tapping is not only a quicker way of conveying an enemy's location, but is sometimes the last thing you're able to do before you're killed. In this instance, being able to provide a rough idea of the direction of enemy fire can be a huge help to your allies, even if you're killed in the process. Plus, with the game offering a chance to return to the fight, you may be dropped back into the fray anyway.

In fact, the Ping system works in death, even if only to identify your corpse so your banner can be retrieved for revival. If you survived an encounter but your health is low and you have no healing items, requesting them from your squad is as easy as pressing the heal button (D-pad Up on Xbox One and PlayStation 4, 4 on PC), provided they survived, of course. You can also open the healing menu by holding the healing button.

Choices

For more granular control of your callouts, holding the Ping button will bring up a radial menu. This can offer commands such as "I'm covering this area", or "I'm looting over here". It's an extra layer, which can offer more

tactical depth, but it's just as likely you'll earn wins without anything more than a single press or double-tap.

A word of caution, however: while the Ping system is an excellent tool and can easily be the difference between an early exit and reaching the hallowed status of Champion, it can be easy to distract your squad with incessant suggestions of where to go. Be mindful of their needs – if they're not in need of armour, don't Ping every Level 1 helmet on the map. Likewise, it can be easy to accidentally

The Ping menu offers more callout options

double-tap the Ping button and get your squad preparing for an enemy that may not exist. There's cautious, then there's remaining entrenched in an area because one of you THOUGHT you saw a sniper.

Apex Legends' focus on teamwork sets it apart, and the Ping system is key to this. Using it to keep a team supplied and informed should end in success.

TEAMWORK

Apex Legends is built on squad-based gameplay. Read on for tips on turning your ragtag squad into Champions

Apex Legends stands apart from other Battle Royale titles by being strongly focused on teamwork. While it's possible to head off as a lone wolf, you're encouraged to stick with your squad. Co-ordinated teams will always be stronger together, so here are some tips to maximise your squad's efficiency. When picking your character, find one that complements your team's composition. It's a good idea to have a healer, so Lifeline is a solid choice, but other characters are impressive when combined, There are dozens of combinations, and experience will dictate a lot of choices, but don't be afraid to try new things!

Jumping
Once you jump from the dropship, stick with your Jumpmaster until you're close to the ground. Splitting off too early can make it tough to

SQUAD ELIMINATED

Killed By
ManSnowThe

[ManSnowThe]

70

KILLS
997

DAMAGE DONE
242965

SEASON 1 KILLS
178

Not what your
team wants to see

judge your landing location, and the last thing you want is to be isolated from your squad when other teams are prowling. On a similar note, while you're looting separate buildings (to maximise the speed of item collection), try not to overreach. It can be easy to succumb to the temptation of Supply Bins in the distance, only to realise you've put a lot of ground between yourself and your cohorts. Lastly, if you're some way from the first Ring, using the red

balloons to redeploy is a risk. Try to space out your climb to the top, simply to avoid any snipers looking to hit you on your way up.

Loot

Looting is a key component of any Battle Royale, but Apex Legends' focus on squadding up means spreading loot among the three of you is crucial. After all, who'll save you when both of your teammates are unarmed? On that note, be sure to Ping items for collection by other players, and try to honour the "dibs". It can be easy to grab every attachment in a panic, but if it can't be equipped on your weapons, chances are one of your teammates can find a better use for it. A good habit to get into is

12 IN DROPSHIP

281

Stick with your Jumpmaster in the air

opening the map when the first Ring is marked and Pinging an indicator for your squad to the edge of it as it can be easy to miss the dialogue about the circle because you're swapping between two weapon scopes.

being close to your team and being TOO close. There's nothing worse than huddling together, only to all be hit by Gibraltar's airstrike or a well-placed grenade. Similarly, flanking is a double-edged sword: while it's incredibly satisfying to eliminate a squad with a smart pincer movement, remember that because there are only three of you, at least one member of a squad will be alone. It's no good getting the enemy in your scope if you're in the firing line of another team you hadn't spotted.

Position

This brings us onto positioning. While most of the killing is done with firearms, positioning is just as important as pulling the trigger. There's a fine balance between

Care

As the player count ticks down and the map gets smaller, consider deploying Lifeline's Care Package (her ultimate ability), which can provide excellent tools for the final battle. Of course, it takes time to deploy and will give away your position, so try to use it in the downtime between the Ring shrinking.

Revival

If a teammate is downed, don't panic. Reviving a teammate in a rush can lead to two unnecessary deaths – reviving doesn't take long, but it will leave you exposed. Of course, if you managed to spread out the loot, there's a chance they'll be able to use a knockdown shield, which can be the difference between a whole squad being eliminated or pulling it back from the brink. If you see an enemy attempting a finisher on your teammate, don't forget that these can be interrupted – often fatally.

If you have Wraith on your team, consider creating a portal near a downed teammate so they can limp to safety, or use Bangalore's smoke grenade to allow your team to revive, heal and reposition.

Banner

Of course, there's always the chance your teammate will be finished off. But if you can deposit a player's banner at a respawn point, you'll be able to call them back in. Collecting a banner is quick, but does involve a moment where you're unable to fire, so try not to get cornered. Respawn points are scattered across the map, but try to find one with some loot

nearby ready for your revived teammate to pick up. Failing that, you'll have to share some of your weaponry and ammo.

With any luck, you've got three teammates left and you're approaching the final battle. Depending on where the Ring ends up, this may be flat ground or somewhere with plenty of cover. One of the best plans of action is to linger on the outskirts of the circle and locate any competitors, so fan out and cover a certain area, with some overlap between you. If you have grenades, use them to flush out enemies, preferably with a high throwing arc to hide their origin. Just keep the "close vs too close" warning in mind so you're not undone by a swarm of grenades from enemies that have outfoxed you.

The joy of Apex Legends is that there are plenty of strategies being developed all the time. Play to your strengths, and always focus on supporting your teammates. It's the only way to victory.

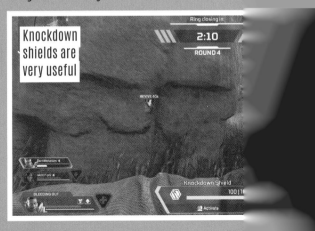

Knockdown shields are very useful

ARMED & DANGEROUS!

Know the weapons of Apex...

Plenty of loot can be picked up on the battlefield. The map is littered with Supply Bins, crates and enemies to murder and steal from. However, it can be difficult to know what each item does and which weapons are worth grabbing. With that in mind, here's a look at all the weapons and other items you can pick up on your travels through Kings Canyon.

Just remember that landing in any of the map's Hot Zones or on the Supply Ship circling the map will offer the best loot, but be prepared to fight for it!

Also, try to pick two weapons that use separate ammo types – that way, if you run out of ammo for one, you'll still have some left for another.

Weapons

At the time of writing, there are 20 firearms to choose from. Some are definitely more useful than others (looking at you, Mozambique), but most are deadly in the right hands.

If you're looking to attack enemies from range, remember to allow for bullet drop!

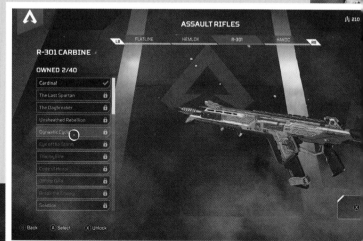

VK-47 Flatline

ASSAULT RIFLE

Ammo Type Heavy

A decent assault rifle for close to mid-range firefights, the VK-47 is ideal in the early game as it rips through shields and health. Attachment options include scopes, an extended heavy mag and a stock – combine all three and you'll be ready to rumble.

Hemlok Burst AR

ASSAULT RIFLE

Ammo Type Heavy

Another assault rifle that uses heavy ammo, but fires in three-round bursts. Attachment options are identical to the VK-47, plus a barrel stabiliser. It's accurate, but only holds 18 bullets.

R-301 Carbine

ASSAULT RIFLE

Ammo Type Light

A fully automatic assault rifle, the R-301 has been a regular in Apex Legends, and the earlier Titanfall gaming franchise. A good all-round weapon, it excels at close to mid-range. Attachment options are a barrel stabiliser, optics, an extended light mag and standard stock.

Havoc

ASSAULT RIFLE

Ammo Type Energy

The Havoc uses energy ammo and requires a brief charge before firing. While you can attach a standard optic or stock to it, look out for the Turbocharger Hop-Up.

Devotion
LIGHT MACHINE GUN
Ammo Type Energy

Capable of hurling a torrent of ammunition at an enemy squad, the Devotion has a very high rate of fire once it gets going. You can change that with the Turbocharger Hop-Up, and other attachment options are standard optics and stock, as well as a barrel stabiliser.

M600 Spitfire
LIGHT MACHINE GUN
Ammo Type Heavy

The Devotion's slightly slower - but more powerful - brother, the Spitfire holds fewer rounds, but they're heavy ammo and so hit harder. It fares slightly better at range too. No Hop-Ups are available, but the magazine can be extended, while other attachment options are standard optics, a barrel stabiliser and standard stock.

Alternator
SUB-MACHINE GUN
Ammo Type Light

A ferocious weapon in close-quarters battles, the Alternator loses most of its bite the further you are from your opponent. Its recoil can be unwieldy, so try to attach a stock or barrel stabiliser. You can also fit a standard optic.

Prowler Burst PDW
SUB-MACHINE GUN
Ammo Type Heavy

The Prowler fires five-round bursts, and since they're heavy they can do significant damage. Add the Selectfire Receiver Hop-Up to go fully automatic. Extending the mag and adding a scope and stock make it a great all-rounder.

Sub-Machine Gun
ASSAULT RIFLE
Ammo Type Light

A firecracker of a weapon, the R-99 blows through its 18-round clip with pace, but its reliance on light ammo means you must be accurate. In tight spaces, this can be ideal, but further away you're better off using something else, even with a stock, extended mag, barrel stabiliser and scope.

Triple Take
SNIPER RIFLE
Ammo Type Energy

A sniper rifle that fires three shots in one may seem like overkill. The Triple Take's horizontally spread shot pattern is perfect for players learning to aim ahead of a target, and the way you can fit a normal or sniper scope allows it to have some use in mid-range fights too.

G7 Scout
SNIPER RIFLE
Ammo Type Light

A sniper rifle in a Battle Royale can feel like manna from heaven, but the G7 Scout is disappointing from distance. Add a normal scope instead of a sniper one, extend the mag and fit a stabiliser and it makes a decent semi-automatic rifle for mid-range combat.

Longbow DMR
SNIPER RIFLE
Ammo Type Heavy

The Longbow deals hefty damage. It also features a bunch of attachment options: barrel stabilisers, extended heavy mag, sniper stock and the option for normal or sniper optics.

Kraber .50-CAL Sniper

SNIPER RIFLE

Ammo Type Unique

A Legendary weapon, the Kraber is rare but deadly. It comes with eight shots split between two mags, and while it doesn't offer any attachment options, it already has a variable scope. In the right hands, it can easily eliminate a whole team.

Mozambique Shotgun

SHOTGUN

Ammo Type Shotgun shells

Our first shotgun is undoubtedly the bottom of the class, becoming meme fodder since Apex's release. It can deal significant damage from close range, but only holds three shells. This can make it difficult if you don't get close enough to kill an enemy by the time you need to reload. Shotgun bolts and a scope are your attachment options.

Peacekeeper

SHOTGUN

Ammo Type Shotgun shells

The Peacekeeper is devastating at close range. It offers six shells per clip, and the spread of shots is tight enough to feel accurate while being wide enough to allow for a margin of error. You can add the Precision Choke Hop-Up to reduce spread, and a scope or shotgun bolt are also options.

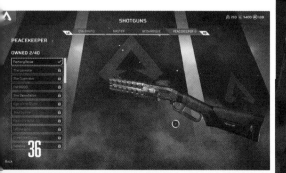

EVA-8 AUTO

SHOTGUN

Ammo Type Shotgun shells

The EVA offers less damage than the Peacekeeper, but in being able to fire so quickly it negates this disadvantage. You can add a standard optic and a shotgun bolt.

Mastiff
SHOTGUN
Ammo Type Unique

A Legendary shotgun, the Mastiff doesn't have any attachment options and doesn't need them. It can kill in one headshot if you're up close, but with four rounds per mag you've got room for error.

Wingman
PISTOL
Ammo Type Heavy

The Wingman is regarded as the best pistol, thanks to its high damage output. Headshots can require a learning curve, but it's worth putting in the time, particularly with the Skullpiercer Hop-Up in place.

RE-45
PISTOL
Ammo Type Light

A rapid-firing fully automatic pistol, the RE-45 can be perfect for hunting players who have just landed. Just use it before they get themselves armour or a better weapon! Attachment options are a barrel stabiliser, standard optic and extended mag.

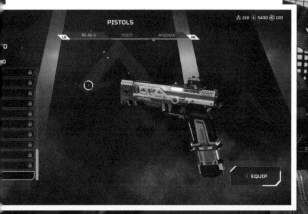

P2020
PISTOL
Ammo Type Light

A very "vanilla" weapon, the P2020 is ideal for the early game, but its influence wanes very quickly. Extending the mag and adding a scope may increase its utility, but you'll be better off saving them for something superior.

UPGRADE YOUR WEAPONS!

Attachments are auto-equipped where possible to your weapons and come in different rarities, from Common to Legendary. Their effects are pretty substantial so you'd be wise to seek them out...

Effects are more profound the rarer the attachment, so a purple Epic stock will reduce drift more than a blue Rare one.

SCOPES offer increased zoom capabilities and come in different variations. Some offer variable zoom, making them ideal for more than one type of combat.

BARREL STABILISERS reduce recoil and are great for rapid-firing weapons to ensure accuracy can be maintained even as bullets are flying.

MAGAZINES offer increased ammunition capacity within a weapon, so hit reload once you've fitted one to make sure it's full. They also speed up reloading as a nice bonus.

SHOTGUN BOLTS, needless to say, can only be fitted to shotguns. They increase their rate of fire, allowing you to get more shots off quickly.

STOCKS reduce weapon drift, making it easier to track a target whilst firing a gun. Used in conjunction with barrel stabilisers, they can make any unruly weapon bend to your will.

Hop-Ups

As we mentioned in the weapons descriptions on the previous pages, some firearms can use special mods known as Hop-Ups. Only one may be attached at any time, but they offer some fairly decent upgrades and can improve the efficiency of your weapon. They only come in Epic rarity, though, so keep your eyes peeled. Opposite is a list of Hop-Ups at the time of writing, along with the weapons they can be used on and what they do.

SELECTFIRE RECEIVER
Prowler Burst PDW and Havoc
Allows for fully automatic fire.

PRECISION CHOKE
Peacekeeper and Triple Take
Charges shots to reduce spread when aiming down the sights.

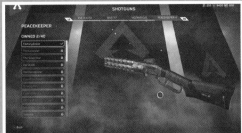

TURBOCHARGER
Havoc and Devotion
Removes required charging before firing.

SKULLPIERCER RIFLING
Longbow DMR and Wingman
Increases headshot damage multiplier.

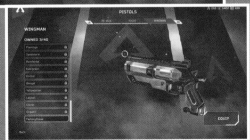

100 | 100

ARMOUR AND HEALING

Increase your chances of surviving until the end of a match with our guide to armour and healing items

Armour

It isn't all offensive pickups in Apex Legends. Armour comes in four rarities too, and is just as important as what you're firing.

The table below shows each item and how their bonuses stack up, all the way to Legendary. These gold items are identical in statistics to their Epic purple counterparts, but feature a unique bonus. Make the most of them, and you'll be almost unstoppable.

Healing

If you've been tagged by an enemy, you'll want to heal yourself. Grab plenty of healing items during a match, because even if you don't need them, you can donate them to a teammate who does.

	Common (White)	Rare (Blue)	Epic (Purple)	Legendary (Gold)
Body Armour	Protects against 50 damage	Protects against 75 damage	Protects against 100 damage	Fully restored when performing a finisher
Knockdown Shield	Protects against 100 damage	Protects against 250 damage	Protects against 700 damage	Allows for a single self-revive
Helmet	30% less headshot damage	40% less headshot damage	50% less headshot damage	Reduced cooldowns on character abilities
Backpack	2 extra inventory slots	4 extra inventory slots	6 extra inventory slots	Reduces time taken to use healing and shield items

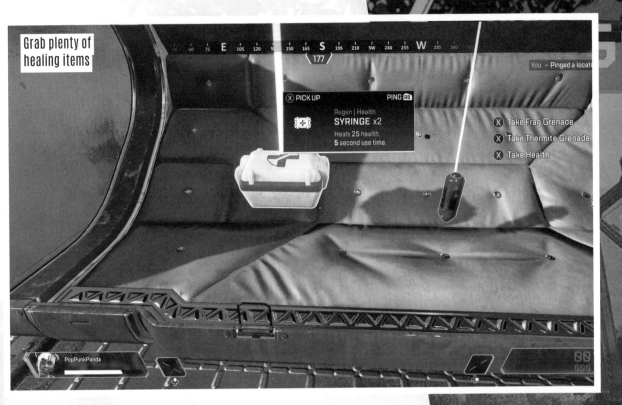

Grab plenty of healing items

X PICK UP   PING RB

Regen | Health
SYRINGE x2
Heals 25 health.
5 second use time.

X Take Frag Grenade
X Take Thermite Grenade
X Take Health

You - Pinged a locat

PopPunkPanda

Since players have both health and shields to manage, there are items that target each one.

On the health side, syringes and med-kits are the order of the day. The former will add 25 points of health and can be applied quickly, while the latter takes more time to apply but can heal 100 points.

Shield pickups are similar: shield batteries will quickly recharge your shield by 25 points, while shield cells take longer to work but help you recover 100 points.

If you're really lucky, you may find an Epic item called a Phoenix Kit. This will both heal you AND restore your shields by 100 points. Just remember that it's slow to apply and leaves you vulnerable until it's fully used. There's no point healing yourself if you end up eliminated, so keep an eye out for a safe spot.

The final pickup you can find is the Ultimate Accelerant. This Rare item knocks 20% off of your ultimate ability's cooldown time, which can be handy in a pinch or when you're approaching the final battle.

The Phoenix Kit will heal both you AND your shields

SUPPLY AND

Time to get out there and gear up! But where best to look? Follow our handy tips

◆ N E Person7

You won't do too well walking into a group of enemies with just your fists, so gearing up is imperative for survival. Guns, armour and other helpful items litter the map, and splitting them among you and your teammates is not only incredibly important, but highly rewarding.

While loot distribution is mostly randomised in a match, there are ways to maximise your haul. Use these handy tips to give yourself a big advantage on the battlefield.

designated Hot Zone we talked about earlier, featuring high-tier weapons and grade A loot. Here you'll be able to snag weapons with attachments, plenty of ammo and higher rarity armour than in other areas on the map.

Of course, as is the case with most Battle Royale titles, everything is a calculated risk. The Hot Zone is marked on the map for every player to see, which can lead to a huge number of squads converging on one spot. This

Hot Zones

While you're in the dropship, open up your map and look out for the highlighted blue area. This is the

Few things are more satisfying than an unopened Supply Bin

N E Person7

⏣ SUPPLIES

Spot that Hot Zone?

MAP FEATURES

⬡ Respawn Beacon
Bring banner to revive dead squad members

⬡ Supply Ship
High tier loot barge

⬤ Hot Zone
High tier loot zone. Chance for a fully kitted weapon.

⬡ Supply Drop
Chance for high tier loot

Panda

DEMAND

Sonic28092001

00 [Finisher] Kingmurre

Death Racer92

Ry5taR [Finisher] YaKuZa2K8

certainly isn't ideal for new players, and it can lead to a short match for those who aren't first to the loot.

Supply Ships

There are alternatives. A Supply Ship floats above certain parts of the map, and it too features overpowered weaponry. Again, there's a catch: the ship is constantly moving, so you'll need to aim for it from the jump. Since there are stacks of weapons to choose from, loads of other squads will be working to grab them too. Survive, and you'll be holding a pile of first-rate weaponry and can jump from the ship – Apex Legends has no falling damage, so you'll be safe.

Someone has been here, so be careful!

Supply Bins

Once you're out in the wild, Supply Bins are your best friends. These white and red boxes will contain anything from guns, ammo, throwable weapons, and even armour and health icons. Thankfully, because they're so large, it can be easy to see when they've been opened, and Pinging this information will inform your teammates that someone has been nearby.

Apex Packs

While exploring, you may also unearth an Apex Pack. These emit a sound when you're nearby, and tend to be in the corner of a room or hard to reach places. These are colour-coded according to the level of loot inside, which is usually good.

Finally, you'll receive notifications about Supply Drops. These fall from the sky and hold three pieces of high-level loot, and are often found in the middle of firefights. It can be tempting to work your way to them, but do so at your peril, as their location is sent to enemies too, and they often land where there's little to no cover.

With these tips, you should find plenty of toys to play (and kill) with. Now there's just the small matter of outlasting 19 other teams and bringing home the win. Thankfully, we have faith in you!

BACK FROM THE DEAD

Often it can feel like all is lost. How do you pull your team back from the brink of defeat?

As with all the best-laid plans, there are times when things don't quite go right. Like when you're running into a conflict with two comrades who are cut down, leaving you solo on the battlefield. In many Battle Royale titles, this would be considered the time to wave a white flag, certainly for your downed teammates, who may not want to spectate your view for the next few engagements until you find yourself outnumbered.

Thankfully, Apex Legends features a respawn system as well as the revive

Revive your teammate quickly

PopPunkPanda

system used by other games in the genre. The important distinction is that when a teammate is downed, they can be revived. Respawning requires more time and effort, but we'll cover both here.

If a squad member is incapacitated in a match, they'll fall to the floor and be unable to use their weapons. In this instance, their only defence will be a knockdown shield (if they picked one up), and they'll move very slowly. Needless to say, it isn't a good position to be in, and enemies can add insult to injury by using a stylish (but risky) finishing move.

Revive

When a player is down in this way, and providing it's safe to approach them, they can be revived via a button prompt. It's a fairly quick process, but

it does leave you open to attack. Lifeline's revives take 25% less time to complete, and once a player is revived they'll have access to all of their previously held loot.

Remember there's a time limit to reviving somebody, so try not to faff around too much! You'll also want to find some health items to be able to restore any lost vitality – reviving isn't an instant fix.

Of course, if an enemy gets to your friend before you do, things end a little differently. Once your teammate has been killed (RIP,

Remember there's a time limit to reviving somebody

You - P

X Pick up DL

45

Respawn Beacons are large and red

Hold Ⓧ Use the Respaw

PopPunkPanda

18

R-301 P2020

Grab a downed teammate's banner

SPACE PING NEAREST RESPAWN BEACON

Look for a Spawn Beacon surrounded by Supply Bins

friend), you can grab a "banner" from the loot box they drop upon death. The animation is fairly snappy, but again will leave you vulnerable. Once you have the banner, check your map to locate a Respawn Beacon. These will allow you to deposit the banner, calling in a dropship to transport your fallen comrade back to the field. A word of warning, however – they'll land back in Kings Canyon with none of their previously assembled gear. No weapons, attachments, armour or healing items.

60   75   E   105   120   Ping

Bangalore's smoke grenade can break line of sight

Respawn Beacon

With that in mind, it's worth looking for a Respawn Beacon that is further from the centre of the next Ring, preferably surrounded by Supply Bins. Doing so gives your revived teammate an opportunity to defend themselves, rather than simply hide in a bush while you have all the fun.

These beacons are large and red, and have a green projection of the dropship on them. Depositing a banner in a Respawn Beacon is time-consuming, so ensure a teammate covers you. Of course, if you're the last member of your team alive, just try to make sure you're not being watched. Savvy enemies will camp around these beacons, looking to pick off players trying to call in their comrades.

If you do happen to be the last person standing in your team, do your best to escape any entanglements. You'll be a sitting duck against a roving pack of players, so making yourself scarce is key.

To that end, some Legends have it easier than others. Bangalore's smoke grenade can be a great way to break line of sight and allow for a tactical retreat. Wraith's portal is also perfect for hot-tailing it out of the sights of the enemy, while using something like Gibraltar's aerial Mortar Strike ultimate ability can buy a few valuable seconds.

There are few things more satisfying than turning a match around by calling in two of your allies, restocking with fresh gear, and heading back out onto the killing fields to secure the win.

MOVING QUICKER!

Give yourself the edge and discover how to get around the map faster

Apex Legends has a pretty sizeable map. You can get around most of it in a single match, but there are ways to travel that bit faster. It's important to note, though, that every Legend runs at exactly the same speed!

Holstering

One of the key things Apex Legends teaches you in its tutorial mode is if you have your weapon armed and primed, you're going to move slightly slower. To get up to top running speed, you need to holster your weapon. You'll move 10-15% faster than if you have it ready.

Sliding

We love the sliding mechanic, which is perfect when you're at the top of a big hill and need to get to the bottom quickly. In instances

Red balloons fire you into the air

Holster your weapon to run quicker

like that, it's faster than running. Just think before you slide, though, as sometimes it's quicker to run, especially on flat ground. The trick to moving fast on foot is to combine sliding AND running. Note that when you're sliding, you become much harder to hit, so there's an advantage beyond just building up a bit of extra speed.

Slide and jump

Jumping doesn't tend to slow you down too much, and it's quicker than you may think to leap to higher ledges, climb walls and the like. The paciest use of jumping comes when you combine it with sliding. It's best to stick your weapon away, then slide as normal. Just as you think you're going to slow down, take a leap forwards. You'll land on the ground running again, and do so for a second or two to get your speed back up. Now go straight into another slide. Repeat as often as you need!

Ziplines

These are dotted around the canyon and make travelling between areas on the map far quicker. Horizontal ziplines get you quickly from one place to another at roughly equal heights. Vertical ziplines work in the same way, only they get you to a higher or lower position. Then there are balloons. These can be really useful. You quickly ascend straight up in the air, then when you get to the top and jump off, the rockets you deploy at the start of every match are activated again. This can be hugely useful for covering large areas of ground quickly. The downside of using ziplines is you tend to be easy to spot, so bear that in mind.

One more thing on moving around: you may have played Fortnite before, and be used to jumping around all the time to make yourself a harder target. That doesn't work so well in Apex Legends, and in fact tends to have the opposite effect: you make yourself stand out more!

> **When you're sliding, you become much harder to hit**

Ziplines make travelling quicker

ROUND 1 - CLOSING   1:26

Apex Legends wants you to play as a team, but to some players, kills are everything – and for good reason

GETTING KILLS!

The logic in hunting for more is pretty obvious: the more kills you have, the more XP you earn, which helps you level up faster for the Battle Pass and in general. With that in mind, who wouldn't want to get as many kills as possible?

However, getting kills is actually harder than it looks. For one, you want to get them without actively shooting your teammates in the back and leaving them for dead, but you also don't want to do everything for your team. After all, they deserve a challenge too.

So we've put together some great tips that will help you to rack up your kill count without dooming your teammates.

Positioning

The Kings Canyon map is huge, so you're bound to find some nooks and crannies your team can hide behind or squeeze in to surprise the enemy. While running and gunning can lead to kills, why not take a different route (usually the higher ground) and drop in, surprise, then kill your enemy before they even realise you're there?

So the next time the enemy runs into a building, try to get at them from the roof instead of following them in, as it could be a trap.

Setting traps

Each Legend has a range of abilities that can help you to escape or give you a leg-up in a fight. Some can even do both if used correctly. For example, you can pull enemies

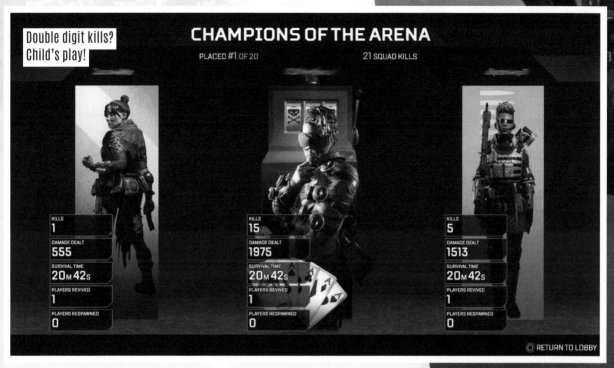

Double digit kills? Child's play!

CHAMPIONS OF THE ARENA

PLACED #1 OF 20   21 SQUAD KILLS

	KILLS	DAMAGE DEALT	SURVIVAL TIME	PLAYERS REVIVED	PLAYERS RESPAWNED
	1	555	20M 42S	1	0
	15	1975	20M 42S	1	0
	5	1513	20M 42S	1	0

○ RETURN TO LOBBY

towards you with Pathfinder's grapple, or lure enemies into a trap with Wraith's teleport or Mirage's decoys.

Similarly, firing your gun, using Lifeline's Care Package, Bangalore's smoke grenade and the like can bait enemies into believing you're in one place, when you're actually nowhere nearby. This allows you to strategically reposition and take your enemy by surprise.

Weapons skills

Picking up a weapon and not knowing how it works is a sure way to get killed. It may get you out of trouble if you're just starting a match, but during the middle and end? Your enemies will likely be equipped with a weapon they know and trust. This puts them at an advantage over you, the person who doesn't quite know how the weapon they're handling works.

Get to know your weapon: remember its fire rate and what accessories work effectively with it. Once you find a handful of guns that suit you, you'll be more confident knowing which ones to look for in future matches.

Not knowing how your weapon works will get you killed

Charging in

If you're by yourself, with no shield or health kits, it should be obvious that you're going to be destroyed by the enemy. However, if you're confident in your aim and team composition, and have a supply of health and shields, rushing at the enemy team isn't such a bad idea. Also, if you've knocked all but one of the enemy team down, don't hesitate! That could give time for teammates to be revived, evening the odds. Who wants that? Not you!

Run at gunfire

One of the most boring things in Apex Legends is running around collecting gear, but not coming across anyone you can use it on. That's why, as scary as it may sound, if you hear gunshots, you should always run towards them, and not just because you want to sate your boredom. Running into danger forces you to think smart and puts you in a situation where you have to fight.

Besides, if you want kills, you most definitely shouldn't be running away from the action. Yes, you may well die a few times, but once you get the hang of things, you'll be Kill Leader before you know it.

> If you hear gunshots, you should run towards them

If you can, take the high ground

Use grenades

Gunning down your enemies may well feel infinitely more satisfying, but there are moments where your guns or your abilities simply won't be enough. This is particularly true at the start of a match, where the only weapons you may have are your grenades, arc stars and thermite.

While grenades can be useful for killing an enemy team, they're also pretty good at herding the enemy where you want them to go so you can finish them off. Thermite in particular is excellent at doing that, as getting hit by it will give you continuous damage for a few seconds after.

Communicate

Apex Legends is a team-based Battle Royale, so it shouldn't be a surprise to you that, to be at your most effective, you'll need to communicate with your teammates. You can do that through Pinging or, if you're feeling particularly brave and want to risk talking to people on the internet, through your headset.

Talking can be helpful, as you not only get the opportunity to tell your team an enemy is nearby, but also what you plan to do. When everyone knows where you are and what your plan is, you and your team's synergy increases. The end result could be that you all have more chance of getting kills.

A team that talks gets more kills

Headshots

It may seem obvious, but many people don't aim for the head when they have the chance. Adrenaline can kick in, and you end up popping off bullets against their body instead, which damages them, but not enough to down them almost immediately.

Moving left and right can make getting headshots a lot harder, but after several goes it will become as natural as breathing. So remember, always aim for the head!

PUZZLE PAGES

Test you brain again with these teasers

VIS-QUIZ

AN ARM GAS
(Anagrams)

Here are some tricky Apex Legends characters, items and places for you to de-jumble

All the answers for these puzzles can be found on page 92. No cheating, though!

Brag Alone

Clue: Indian Legendary?

_ _ _ _ _ _ _ _ _

Blast Spate

Clue: A season of shooting

_ _ _ _ _ _ _ _ _ _

Tribal Rag

Clue: A rocky character

_ _ _ _ _ _ _ _ _

Zen Hoot

Clue: Prepare before you go there

_ _ _ _ _ _ _

Conga Skinny

Clue: This one is big and wide

_ _ _ _ _ _ _ _ _ _ _

Nil I Feel

Clue: A medical Legendary

_ _ _ _ _ _ _ _ _

Phat Friend

Clue: A scout, no doubt

_ _ _ _ _ _ _ _ _ _

Token Hip Xi

Clue: Helping you rise from the ashes

_ _ _ _ _ _ _ _ _ _

Egor Carb Hunt

Clue: Makes you faster

_ _ _ _ _ _ _ _ _ _ _ _

World Niftier

Clue: A season of fun

_ _ _ _ _ _ _ _ _ _ _

SUPPLY DROP TIPS

You may have played Battle Royale games before, where Supply Drops come from the sky to allow you to tool up in the middle of a match. Apex Legends works slightly differently. There are Supply Drops, but there are also Supply Ships, so let's look at both.

Drops

A common feature of Battle Royale titles, Supply Drops are sent to the ground during a match. In the case of Apex Legends, they arrive in pods and, as with games like Fortnite, you get advance warning one is on the way – in this case, a blue ripple on the screen.

It's worth keeping an eye out for them too. Supply Drops contain three different pieces of loot, and it tends to be very good stuff. Often amazingly good stuff, including – potentially – Legendary weapons. In fact, you can only get your paws on two of the very best weapons in the game this way – the Mastiff shotgun and the Kraber.50 CAL sniper rifle. Both of these can take out a fully armoured opponent with a single shot, so competition tends to be pretty hot for them!

Some of the best weapons can only be found in drops

Ships

Supply Ships slowly work their way across the map, first appearing at the start of any match. They're worth looking out for as they hold plenty of top-quality loot. Be warned, though, that they inevitably make for popular places as people have the same idea and look to kit up nice and early.

If you're successful in landing on the ship – and you can do so as you rocket onto the map – and subsequently bagging its contents, it puts you in a much smarter position for the rest of the match. It's a very high-risk strategy, though.

Supply Ships reappear throughout a match. They move to their destination on the map, and a zipline is sent to the ground once they get there. As you might expect, you can then zipline up to the ship and have a good look around. Again, they attract lots of attention, even later in the game, so it pays to stay frosty should you choose to climb aboard one.

Supply Ships carry some grade A loot

Top Tip

If you see a Supply Ship, but don't want to risk going aboard, why not wait underneath? Whoever's on board is likely to have taken damage by fighting to get the best loot. As such, once they drop back down to the ground, try to quickly take them out, then nab all the good stuff they've just managed to collect!

COLOUR CODING

Get to grips with the colour coding system quickly

The developers of Apex Legends are well aware that you often have to make decisions in a hurry, so they've implemented a colour coding system to help you make choices in an instant. Note that the colour coding works slightly differently between loot and ammunition types, as we'll explain.

What's rare?

As you'd expect, the game grades the rarity of its items with a colour coding system. It's thus crucial to learn it quickly. The colours are:

White: Common
Blue: Rare
Purple: Epic
Gold: Legendary

Gold items are the trickiest to find. Only two weapons in Season 1 were graded as Legendary from the off: the Mastiff shotgun and Kraber .50-CAL sniper rifle. You'll find them both in Supply Drops.

Other weapons arrive in basic form, and it's the attachments you need to keep an eye out for to upgrade your arsenal. That's where the colour coding system comes firmly into play. The rarer the

Phoenix Kits are purple and restore health AND shields

15 30 NE 60 75 E 105 120

It's a good rule of thumb to seek out purple and gold items

Ammunition

The colour coding of ammunition works slightly differently and doesn't cover rarity at all. In fact, it's colour coded just so you can quickly work out what's what. The colours work as follows:

Brown: Light rounds
Greeny blue: Heavy rounds
Red: Shotgun shells
Yellow: Energy ammunition

attachment, the better the upgrade. Just how effective an upgrade is specifically is a closely guarded secret, with regular updates slightly changing the impact an upgrade can make.

For body shields, knockdown shields, backpacks and helmets, the same colour coding system applies. The rarer the item, the more effective it is.

Watch too for loot chests that are glowing after you've landed a kill. They glow with the colour of the rarest item you'll find inside them, allowing you to quickly choose whether they're worth investigating or not.

More defence

In terms of shields and healing items, colour coding varies. Phoenix Kits are purple and the most effective, as they restore 100 health and shield points. Shield cells and med-kits are blue, restoring 100 shield and health, respectively. Shield batteries and syringes are white and restore 25 points. Be on the lookout for the Ultimate Accelerant – it's blue and will reduce the cooldown time on your ultimate ability.

It's a good rule of thumb to seek out purple and gold items. If you come across ones you already have or don't need, let your squad mates know just what you've found and where they can find it.

THE RIGHT TOOLS
FOR THE JOB

Apex Legends caters to plenty of different playstyles, so it's key to play to your own strengths

Apex Legends offers plenty of weapons, and with assault rifles, SMGs, shotguns, sniper rifles and trusty old pistols, there's plenty of diversity. Of course, that doesn't mean they're all created equally, at least in terms of catering to your own strengths. After all, holding a sniper rifle when you're much better versed in close combat isn't going to help a great deal.

Of course, the following scenarios are ideal, but a lot of the fun is working with what you can find on the battlefield. With that in mind, here are some weapons to

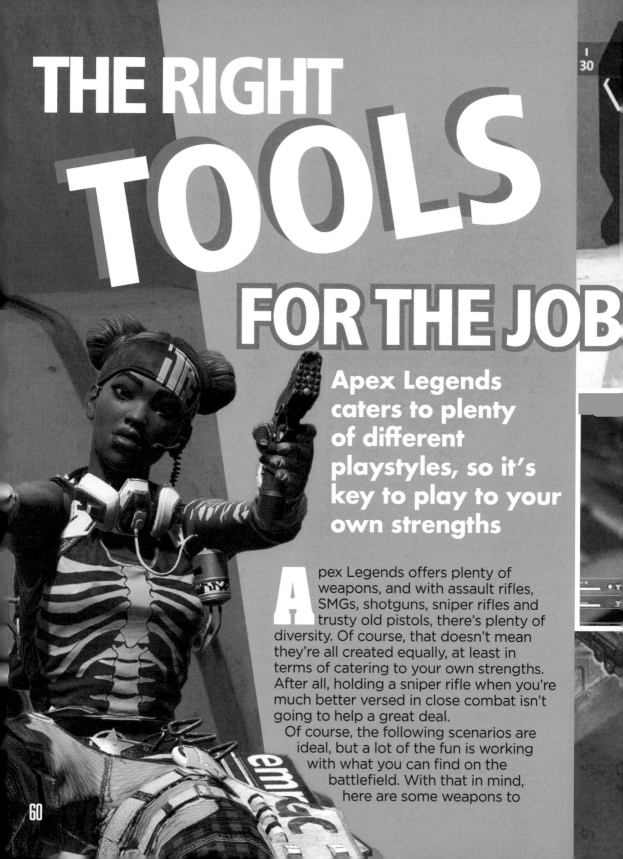

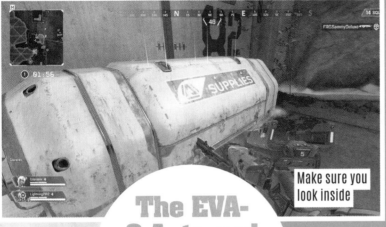

Make sure you look inside

it's accurate, semi-automatic, and with a decent mid-range scope it can be ideal for a variety of engagements at medium range, too. Secondly, all weapons suffer from bullet drop, which you'll have to take into account when engaging enemies at any range, but particularly at long range.

Dream setup

With that in mind, the dream setup is a Longbow DMR with an extended mag and a variable AOG scope. This essentially allows the power and range of a sniper rifle, a scope with two distance options, and enough ammo per mag to account for making a mistake or two due to bullet drop. If you do nail some headshots, having Skullpiercer Rifling will do some serious damage.

The EVA-8 Auto and Peacekeeper are very solid choices

The EVA-8 can rip through doors and enemies

look out for, depending on your playstyle.

It seems obvious to suggest sniper rifles for those who prefer long-distance combat, but there are some considerations. Firstly, the Longbow DMR is probably the best all-round distance weapon:

As fun as it can be to snipe an enemy from across the map, nothing says "Hello" like a shotgun to the chest, and the game has a couple of great options here. While the Mozambique is the subject of memes throughout the community, the EVA-8 Auto and Peacekeeper

Easily the coolest-looking weapon in the game

Grab those attachments!

Keeping a shotgun and a Longbow is a great combo

are incredibly solid choices.

The EVA-8 is an automatic shotgun, and with a shotgun bolt fitted it can pound through doors and enemies with ease. It's devastatingly effective at close range, and paired with a holo scope or Digital Threat scope it's an ideal candidate for the "first through the door" close-combat squad member.

On the other hand, the Peacekeeper is a distinctly slower-paced weapon. It only offers six shells per clip, and being lever operated it doesn't fire as quickly as the EVA-8. Thankfully, it hits like a freight train at close to almost mid-range, allowing you to clear rooms with style. Adding

a Precision Choke Hop-Up, as well as a shotgun bolt, means the Peacekeeper will have a reduced spread and quicker fire.

Keeping a shotgun and a Longbow is a great combo, particularly with the variable AOG scope to cover the mid-range, but it's always nice to keep something with more rounds per minute to react to any ambushes. Thankfully there are a couple of great choices here. While LMGs are powerful and stacked with ammunition, their inaccuracy (and propensity to draw other squads with the sound they produce) make them best for laying down fire while a squad mate flanks around.

SMGs

That leaves submachine guns and assault rifles as the more viable option, and there's one of each that stand out as the best of the bunch. In terms of SMG, the Prowler Burst PDW is a punchy weapon that fires heavy ammo in bursts. With an extended mag and a stock, it's a highly manoeuvrable weapon that sacrifices little in power. Adding the Hop-Up

Selectfire Receiver can make it fully automatic.

On the assault rifle side, the R-301 fires lighter ammo, but is an excellently accurate assault rifle, particularly once equipped with a suite of attachments. If you can't find a barrel stabiliser or a stock, stick to using it in the close to mid-range.

If you're looking for a more accurate assault rifle, the Hemlok's burst fire means hitting a series of headshots can do a lot of damage, particularly as it uses heavy rounds.

> Other than the early game, pistols are highly under-powered

Pistols

Other than the early game, pistols are highly underpowered, with the exception of the Wingman. It's slow, but when it hits, it hits hard. It can use Skullpiercer Rifling too, which can make it devastating if you're accurate enough.

Of course, any mix of the above is going to prove useful, but keep an eye on the ammo types required. The Hemlok, Prowler and Longbow all use heavy rounds, so try to keep one of the three to prevent each weapon dipping into the other's ammo reservoir.

Needless to say, armour is better at higher levels. The same goes for knockdown shields and backpacks. There's little science to finding a solid set of armour – just remember to pick up anything dropped by other competitors.

Hopefully this will give you some ideal loadouts to work towards, but they may not work for you. In that case, experimentation is key until you find the weapon that does work for you – it may even be the Mozambique.

An assault rifle in a smaller form factor

Pistols are only worth using in the early game

SKINS & CUSTOMISATION

◆ N E Person7

Want to stand out on the battlefield? Find out how to customise the game to suit your style

In Apex Legends, Respawn has given you the opportunity to express yourself through a mixture of customisation options. Not just your guns, but the skins your Legend wears and their voice lines too. It may feel like Respawn has taken a leaf out of Overwatch's book, but given how customisable that game is, we're sure no one playing Apex Legends is going to complain.

Here's the full list of customisation options available to you:
- Weapon Skins
- Legend Skins
- Legend Finishers
- Banner Frames
- Banner Poses
- Banner Stat Trackers
- Intro Quips
- Kill Quips

Guns can be given a makeover

UNLOCK

Weapon Skins

These come in four levels of rarity – Legendary, Epic, Rare and Common – and give your guns a shiny new look. They won't affect how the weapons work, though, and are purely cosmetic.

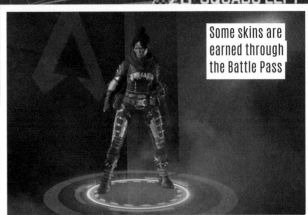

Some skins are earned through the Battle Pass

Legend Skins

These too are broken down into rarities, from Common to Legendary, and will deck out your character in a slick new outfit. Again, they're just for fun and don't impact gameplay.

OWNED 1/3

First Finisher
Existential Crisis
Into the Light

Finishers are Legendary cosmetics

Legend Finishers

These finishing moves allow you to show off your executions and end your downed opponents with style. Most Legends have three different finishers, although some like Octane only have two.

Banner Frames

Banner frames let you further express your style through different layouts, colour schemes and even features like spiderwebs, gas clouds, love hearts, and much more. Some are even animated, so you can get more creative with your in-game look.

Banner Poses

Everyone likes to strike a pose once in a while, and with this customisation option you can pose your favourite Legend in whatever way you think suits them best. Again, some are even animated!

Banner Stat Trackers

If you like to show off your achievements, these banner stat trackers will be just the ticket. You can show both allies and enemies your total kills, kills per season, headshots, and players revived, so they know what you're capable of in a fight.

Intro Quips

Intro quips are used by your Legends when they've just become Champions. You'll hear them as you go into your next match, and are a fun way to not only show what you're about to your teammates, but also to know more about the Legend you're playing.

Kill Quips

Kill quips are similar to intro quips, only you're more likely to hear your opponent's rather than your own. This is because when you've finished killing someone, you're usually too busy trying to snare the loot or get the hell out of dodge!

Obtaining items

One way to grab the cosmetic items on offer is to grind your way through level after level to earn an Apex Pack, which gives you three items from the huge pool of options available. This can be a combination of different cosmetic items, such as a kill quip, a Legend skin and a weapon skin.

Alternatively, the main in-game currency, Apex Coins, can be bought with real money and used to buy Battle Passes, more cosmetic items and even new Legends. Apex Packs can also be acquired this way.

Crafting Metals is another currency that is most commonly used for weapon skins, stat trackers and intro/kill quips, and players can craft the specific cosmetic items they want. This currency is special in that it can only be earned through Apex Packs.

Finally, Legend Tokens are a currency that you earn after increasing your player level. These are easier to get your hands if you don't mind the grind, but can take a heck of a long time, depending on your player level. However, they are useful for unlocking Legends and cosmetics, so we recommend saving them up all the same.

Apex Coins get you cosmetics faster

Rotating Shop

Like most recent Battle Royale games, Apex Legends features an in-game store, where you can purchase extra special Legendary skins for personalising your weapons and characters, current and future Battle Passes, plus Apex Packs to unlock a wealth of cosmetic options.

As the name implies, the shop rotates what it sells every so often, so if you really must have a certain cosmetic item, you're encouraged to buy it sooner rather than later if you don't want to miss out.

Unfortunately, you can only purchase cosmetic items in the shop with Apex Coins, which means you'll either have to grind to get them, or open your wallet and spend hard cash.

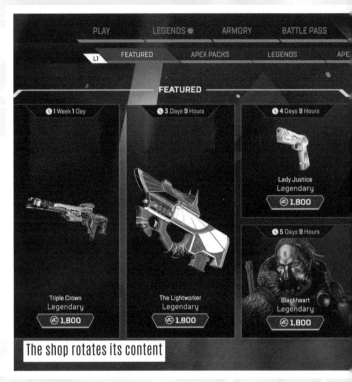

The shop rotates its content

Apex Packs can be bought in store

Can you pay to win?

One thing's clear: Apex Legends wants you to rely on your strengths and abilities, your teammates and your aim, rather than having enough money in your pocket to make yourself a threat.

As far as we know, there are no plans to change this. For now, everything that can be bought is purely cosmetic. So you'll just have to put in the practice and the hours to bag a win, rather than rely on the contents of your wallet.

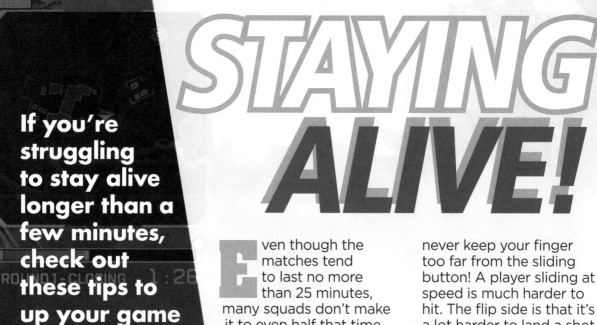

STAYING ALIVE!

If you're struggling to stay alive longer than a few minutes, check out these tips to up your game and survive longer

Even though the matches tend to last no more than 25 minutes, many squads don't make it to even half that time. What, then, are the tricks to staying alive in a round?

Get moving

Basic Battle Royale rules: if you stand still, you're an easier target. Sometimes when you're in good cover, or have a decent height advantage, it's safer to be still. But in most areas of the map, it pays to keep moving, which will increase your chance of staying alive. If you want to move faster – another very useful tactic – then never keep your finger too far from the sliding button! A player sliding at speed is much harder to hit. The flip side is that it's a lot harder to land a shot, but given this is the section on surviving longer, we figured you'd give us a pass on that.

Tactical retreats

Sometimes firefights find you so heavily outnumbered or outgunned (or both!) that the only option is to beat a retreat. This is where some pre-planning helps.

When you go to a built-up area of the map, always have an exit plan in mind. Since you're generally facing squads rather than individuals, this can be easier said than done. Find a zipline, a big hill you can slide down, or somewhere you can move very fast. Also remember that you take no damage when you fall. If you need to jump from a height to get away, just do it!

If you hear a gunfight, move towards it

Timing attacks

To win a match of Apex Legends, you have to get your hands dirty. As such, you can't hide on the outskirts and let teammates do all the work. That doesn't mean that they can't do some of the work for you, though. When you hear a gunfight going on in the distance – assuming your armour, health and weapons are up to scratch – go towards it.

Chances are there's a firefight where two or more squads are taking chunks out of each other. Whichever side emerges intact, they're likely to have taken a fair amount of damage. As such, get in and try to take them out before they have time to heal. You stand a better chance of landing kills.

Team up

It's a cliché, but it's true: you play Apex Legends as a team, and in the majority of cases it will be the squad which plays as one that wins out.

You can win as an individual, but that's not really the point of the game. As such, stay close to your team and work with them. Don't stand side by side – you'll be an easy target – but never be too far away from each other, either.

> You can't hide on the outskirts and let teammates do all the work

Balance

You pick your Legends in turn at the start of each round, and as such, if you're not choosing first, take note of who everyone else has picked. Get a varied team together with characters that complement each other. You can't all play defensive and/or attacking. Mix up the team and its skills.

Ping

You can expect pretty much every other Battle Royale game over the coming years to have some variant of the Ping system that Apex Legends has introduced. It's brilliant and it pays to use it.

Make sure you're constantly chatting to your teammates using the Ping system. If you find good loot, tell them. If you reckon you've found a good place to get to, tell them. If you see a threat... well, you get the idea.

The important thing is that communicating with your team is a real asset in the game. Even if you've been downed and you're awaiting recovery, you can still pinpoint where an enemy is using the Ping system. Get to grips with it quickly, and always share any important information.

> Make sure you are constantly chatting to your team

Make sure you pick a varied team

Gang up

When you get into a firefight, agree who you're going to target and concentrate all of your fire on them. That way, instead of each taking a separate target, you're all ganging up on the same enemy.

The advantage is that you're likely to knock the opposition squad down by one quickly and, as a result, weaken it by a third. The alternative is that you spread yourself thin and rely on the members of your squad each winning their individual firefights. If you team up, you'll take damage, but you'll defeat your opponent that bit quicker (if all goes to plan!).

Revive

Part of being a team is that if you're taken out, it's not necessarily game over. A teammate can revive you if they get to you in time, and even if they don't they can pick up your banner and bring you back to life. A player is down for a reason, however, and you need to deal with the attacking threat first.

The enemy who shot them is likely still in the vicinity and on the lookout for the rest of your squad. Deal with them first: we can't say this strongly enough. You can't save your teammate if you're taken out! Even though the clock is always ticking, you do have a little time to revive someone, so don't rush, and make sure you assess any dangers first.

When you're killed, you leave behind a banner

Banners

Even if it looks like you're done and dusted, there's still your banner. When a player has fallen, their banner is left behind. If that's you, you can Ping teammates to alert them, and they can respawn you by picking it up and taking it to a Respawn Beacon. They're not always easy to find, and it takes a bit of time to respawn a player. As such, surviving members of the squad should treat this in the same way they would a revival: stay alert, and whoever isn't doing the respawning should cover the other.

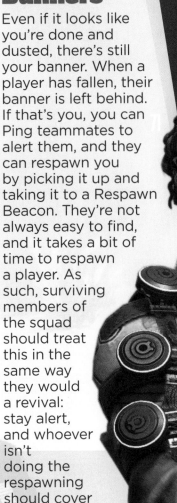

71

UNDERSTANDING DAMAGE

Confused by all the data appearing on screen? Here's how the damage system works

When you shoot at another player in Apex Legends, pay extra attention if your shot hits your opponent. That's because the game will relay some information to you – visually – about just what you're up against!

Firstly, when your shot hits, a number flashes up on screen. This relates to the damage you've done, but the colour of the number that appears is also significant.

If you hit someone and the damage number is red, this is ideal, as it means the opponent you're up against has no armour at all. Assuming they have maximum health, you need to inflict no more than 100 points of damage to knock them down. These are – appreciating not much is easy in Apex Legends – the easiest kills you're ever going to get in the game. However, most of the time, opposing players will have at least some sort of protection, and the numbers will tell you exactly what they have.

Damage number colours are important

- **White means they have Level 1 armour, allowing up to 50 points of extra damage on top of health**
- **Blue means they have Level 2 armour, allowing up to 75 points of damage**
- **Purple means they have Level 3 armour, allowing up to 100 points of damage**

There's also one more colour to look out for. Should the damage report come in yellow, then congratulations! This means you've landed a headshot. Headshots aren't always fatal, as helmets do offer some degree of defence, but they inflict the most damage on an opponent.

The bottom line here is to pay attention: Apex Legends is constantly relaying information that may just give you the upper hand in a fight, so keep a close eye on those damage numbers.

If you hit someone and the damage is red, this is ideal

Maximums

Don't forget that the maximum damage any opponent can take is 200. The maximum health is 100 points, and a further 100 can be added to that via shields. Only Legendary weapons can take down an opponent with maximum points in one hit, so bear in mind that you'll generally need to land a few shots to at least knock a player down.

You'll need to land a few shots to take them down

THE MOST DANGEROUS PLACES

If you're looking for some action and itching for a fight, where's the best spot to land?

If you're on the lookout for a fight pronto, Apex Legends has its fair share of places that should get you into the thick of things fast! Of course, that's not uncommon across Battle Royale games, but what makes Apex a little different is that its map has fewer people on it in the early stages.

Whilst the map is sizeable, the game limits its main match to 60 players, broken into squads of three apiece. In effect, that's 20 squads scattered around the map (given that most squads tend to stick quite closely together).

That means most places in the game are pretty empty, and if you go to the fringes of the map you can go through a match without encountering anyone for quite some time. The flip side is, if you're itching for a fight, there are certain places you need to aim for if you want to come across one quickly!

Supply Ship

The most brutal early firefights in a round are always centred around loot! The first to look out for is the Supply Ship that appears right at the start of a match. If you can land on that, loads of people will be battling to get their mitts on the initial collection of tempting goodies found on board.

Repulsor Station

Some locations are more popular than others

Hot Zone

We can't say this enough: there's pretty much no place more dangerous in a game of Apex than the Hot Zone at the start of a match. You know why by now: just be aware that if you venture there early, you have to be primed and ready. It's not a place for novices to head.

Head to the Hot Zone for a fight

Map locations

Certain spots on the map always seem to attract more players, irrespective of where the Hot Zone appears.

A popular place on the Season 1 map is Hydro Dam. There's no shortage of decent loot here, but what makes it particularly taxing is the environment. You need to be constantly on your guard, as there are tonnes of corners, and it's extremely easy to be taken by surprise. Squads who work as well-oiled teams will fare better here.

Bunker, meanwhile, tends to play host to loads of intense battles, the magnet of that oh-so-magical loot bringing squads quickly in its direction!

Finally, don't overlook Airbase, either. The only problem here is that because it's so isolated, it takes time to get to another area.

And finally...

When the Ring closes in, you're asking for serious trouble and one heck of a firefight if you're just standing out in the open in the midst of things. In fact, the game doesn't get any tougher than this! But then you knew that already, right?

Picking 'em off

It's a sneaky tactic, but a good one. When you're in an area you know is going to be chock-a-block with players searching for loot, hang around and hide on the outskirts. Let them all fight it out, then pick them off one by one when they're weaker. It's still a dangerous game, but it does weigh the odds a little more in your favour!

CHARACTER ABILITIES IN FOCUS

The focus on teamwork is matched only by the game's commitment to characters, so what can they all do?

Each character has three abilities. The first, a passive ability, is in effect at all times, while the second is a tactical ability and operates on a cooldown timer. Finally, each Legend has an ultimate ability, which takes some time to charge.

Bangalore

Bangalore has plenty of tactical options at her disposal, thanks to a kit with plenty of utility. Her passive ability, Double Time, is great for a hasty retreat, as it speeds up her movement when taking fire, especially when used in conjunction with her tactical ability, Smoke Launcher. Using a cloud of smoke to reposition a squad or revive a downed comrade is just as helpful as using it to confuse an enemy squad.

Her ultimate ability, Rolling Thunder, is an artillery barrage, ideal for late-game bombardment of an area if there's not much cover. It not only knocks down enemies, but finishes off downed ones too.

Bloodhound

As the name would suggest, Bloodhound is the tracker of the line-up. Their passive ability allows the player to see recently left footprints, so Bloodhound can stalk them. On the tactical side, Eye of the Allfather reveals all enemies within your line of sight, as well as any traps left by them.

Bloodhound's ultimate ability, Beast of the Hunt, is terrifying. It highlights enemies for a short time, increases movement speed, and essentially turns the player into a killing machine. Use it to sneak up on a squad, and you'll be the Kill Leader in no time.

Bangalore has plenty of tactical options at her disposal

Caustic

The closest thing to a super villain, Caustic is another character with tools that serve multiple purposes. His Nox Gas Trap tactical ability is a gas grenade that will detonate when triggered by an enemy. If they trigger it, his passive ability, Nox Vision, allows him to track enemies within the gas.

His ultimate ability, a Nox gas grenade that covers a significant area, can be used to disorientate or simply eliminate enemies. If you can corner a squad in a building with it, you can easily kill all three if they can't find an exit.

NOTE: Caustic needs to be unlocked using 12,000 Legend Tokens or 750 Apex Coins.

Bloodhound can track recently left footprints

Gibraltar is a great all-round Legend

GIBRALTAR
SHIELDED FORTRESS

Mirage is focused on deception and sleight of hand

Gibraltar

Gibraltar is an excellent all-rounder. His passive ability puts up a shield around his weapon when aiming down the sights, which can be turned on and off, while his tactical ability puts down a dome shield that lasts for 15 seconds. It can be ideal when one player is down, giving a short window of invulnerability to revive them. His ultimate ability begins with a marker being thrown, and a huge mortar strike can deal incredible damage to anyone within its radius.

Lifeline

Lifeline is a great starting character as her kit is easy to understand. Her passive ability quickens the speed of her revive, and healing items take 25% less time to apply. The Heal Drone that forms the tactical part of her repertoire can link to teammates to administer healing. Her ultimate ability drops a Care Package onto the battlefield, containing healing, armour and weapon attachments.

Mirage

A fast-talking trickster, Mirage is focused on deception and sleight of hand. His tactical ability, Psyche Out, sends out a decoy, which is ideal for tricking an opponent you know is watching you from a distance. If they do knock you down, his passive ability, Encore!, will cloak Mirage and send out another decoy. It only lasts for five seconds, but hopefully that's long enough for a teammate to help out.

Mirage's ultimate ability, Vanishing Act, also cloaks him and sends out a handful of decoys to distract (and confuse) opponents.

NOTE: Mirage needs to be unlocked using 12,000 Legend Tokens or 750 Apex Coins.

Octane

The first post-release character, Octane is pretty versatile, and played correctly he can pull enemy team members away from each other with ease. His passive ability, Swift Mend, slowly restores health, while his tactical ability is a Stim shot that increases his movement speed at the cost of his health. Used together, they make him a high-risk, high-reward flanker. His ultimate ability deploys a launch pad that allows a squad to cover a lot of ground very quickly.

NOTE: Octane needs to be unlocked using 12,000 Legend Tokens or 750 Apex Coins.

Pathfinder

A fun character with arguably limited utility, Pathfinder is a cheerful robot. His passive ability highlights the location of the next Ring by scanning a survey beacon. His tactical ability is a grappling hook that can allow for a quick change of position. Unfortunately, his ultimate ability, Zipline Gun, feels one-note. It allows for a speedy escape or a rapid assault, so a team can traverse terrain rapidly.

Wraith

Another well-balanced character with plenty of tactical choice. Her passive ability, Voices From The Void, lets you know when enemies are near, albeit quietly. Her tactical ability, Into The Void, lets her sidestep to another dimension, turning her invisible and preventing damage – perfect for closing the gap or avoiding an ambush. Finally, her ultimate ability, Dimensional Rift, lets you create two linked portals. Your squad can sneak through from one to the other, and it works even if they're downed.

So there you have it, plenty of abilities to learn and form strategies with. Remember that squad composition is important, so it's worth switching characters until you feel comfortable with each.

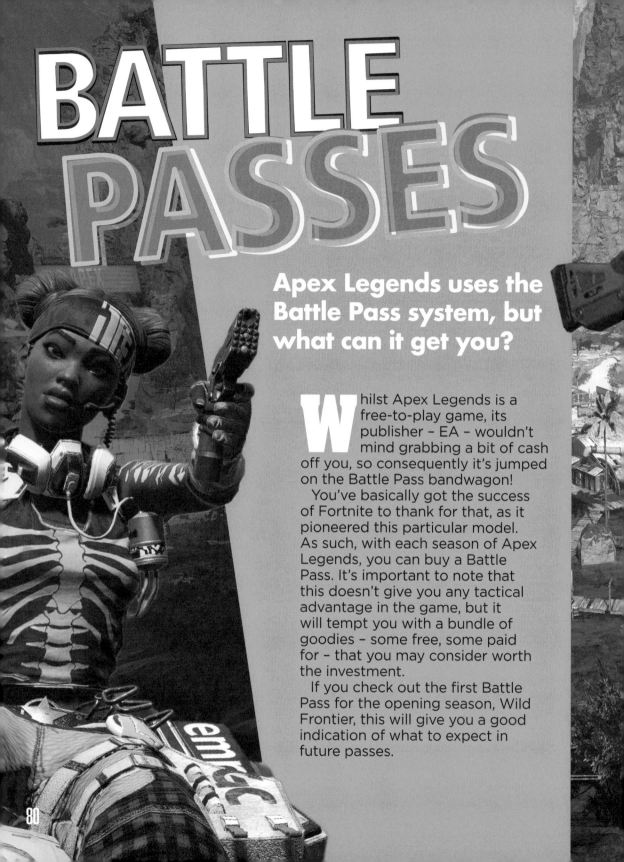

BATTLE PASSES

Apex Legends uses the Battle Pass system, but what can it get you?

Whilst Apex Legends is a free-to-play game, its publisher – EA – wouldn't mind grabbing a bit of cash off you, so consequently it's jumped on the Battle Pass bandwagon!

You've basically got the success of Fortnite to thank for that, as it pioneered this particular model. As such, with each season of Apex Legends, you can buy a Battle Pass. It's important to note that this doesn't give you any tactical advantage in the game, but it will tempt you with a bundle of goodies – some free, some paid for – that you may consider worth the investment.

If you check out the first Battle Pass for the opening season, Wild Frontier, this will give you a good indication of what to expect in future passes.

Won't pay

If you don't fancy parting with any cash, you can get stuff for free in the game by putting in the hours. Season 1 freebies included a Wild Frontier Legend skin, five Apex Packs, and 18 stat trackers. The stat trackers allow you to unlock stats for individual Legends, so you can get a forensic breakdown of how well you've done playing as the character in question. With 20 stats per character at the time of writing, that's a lot to unlock, though.

You earn these freebies by playing through the game and building up your level. You level up by earning XP, and you're rewarded for different things, including:

- How long you survive in a match
- The number of kills and the amount of damage you inflict on opponents
- Taking out the Kill Leader or killing the Champion
- A high-place finish
- Reviving or respawning one of your squad

There are other contributory factors, and it pays to keep an eye on the daily and weekly challenges, which offer XP in return. They'll help to build up to free Battle Pass rewards.

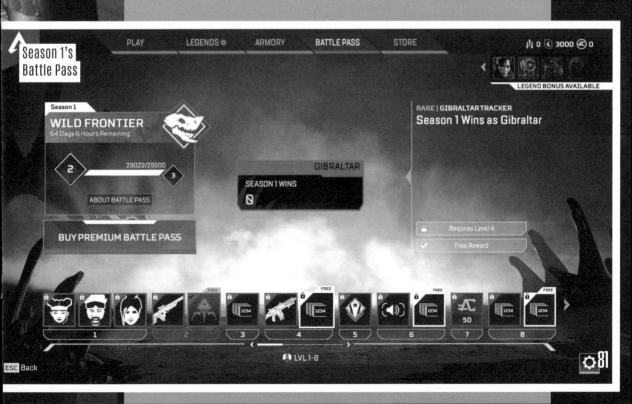

Season 1's Battle Pass

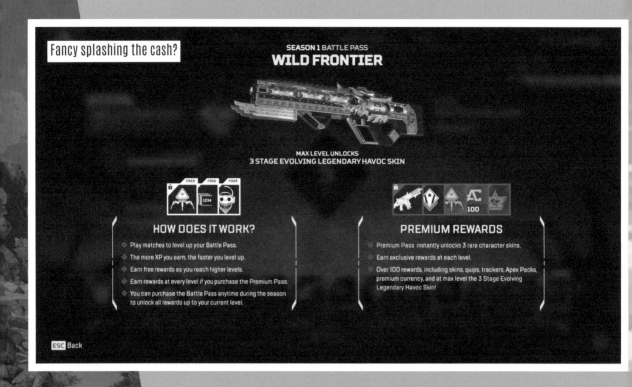

SEASON 1 BATTLE PASS
WILD FRONTIER

MAX LEVEL UNLOCKS
3 STAGE EVOLVING LEGENDARY HAVOC SKIN

FREE   FREE   FREE

HOW DOES IT WORK?

- Play matches to level up your Battle Pass.
- The more XP you earn, the faster you level up.
- Earn free rewards as you reach higher levels.
- Earn rewards at every level if you purchase the Premium Pass.
- You can purchase the Battle Pass anytime during the season to unlock all rewards up to your current level.

PREMIUM REWARDS

- Premium Pass instantly unlocks 3 rare character skins.
- Earn exclusive rewards at each level.
- Over 100 rewards, including skins, quips, trackers, Apex Packs, premium currency, and at max level the 3 Stage Evolving Legendary Havoc Skin!

ESC Back

Will pay

What EA really wants you to do, though, is hand over some of your cash. In exchange for a standard Battle Pass fee of 950 Apex Coins, you'll get access to 100 different rewards. They're all cosmetic, but we have to admit some of them are pretty cool.

When you buy a Battle Pass, you get all the rewards up to and including the level you're currently at in the game. So, if you've earned the XP to reach Level 20, you'll get all the goodies instantly up to that level. And as you work through, you'll receive extra stuff that's exclusive to each individual season of the game. It's a mix of skins, badges, coins, quips, banner frames and more.

The Battle Pass comes with 100 levels for you to work through. And crucially, you can earn enough Apex Coins to pay for the next Battle Pass without having to spend any more hard cash. Whether that strategy continues as Apex Legends becomes more popular remains to be seen.

If you're feeling particularly flush, you can fork out for the premium priced Battle Pass Bundle, which ranges from 2700 to 4800 Apex Coins. The advantage to this is that you instantly unlock the first 25 levels of material. So, if you're currently at Level 31, you'll unlock everything up to Level 56!

Note that everything you pick up as part of a Battle Pass, be it free or paid for, will be carried over into future seasons of the game. Plus, EA is promising that material is exclusive to each season: once a season is done, the extra goodies that came with

> **The plan is for roughly four seasons of Apex Legends each year**

it will no longer be attainable, and you can only keep them if you've earned them in time.

The plan is for roughly four seasons each year, which should equate to four different Battle Passes. Just don't lose sight of the fact that the Battle Pass makes no difference whatsoever to the game. You won't receive an extra weapon that someone without a Pass can't get their hands on.

Extra Legends

Not only are new maps part of the future plan, but new Legends will be introduced too. Octane was the first to be introduced after the game launched, and was added to the roster during the first season. Octane brought along extra abilities, including Stim (being able to move 30% faster for six seconds at a cost of some health), Swift Mend (allowing health to automatically heal over time) and Launch Pad (which allows Octane and/or his teammates to be flung back into the air).

Octane came with a price, though: 750 Apex Coins or 12,000 Legend Tokens. Whether all new Legends will come with such a price tag is unclear right now.

> **One last thing...**
>
> It's worth stressing again that you don't need to buy ANYTHING to play Apex Legends, and you won't be penalised for not doing so. If you can live without the many cosmetic upgrades that come as part and parcel of the Battle Pass, then you can happily play the game without ever handing over a penny!

THE FINAL CHECKLIST

Keep this page open as you head into battle, as we round up the essentials to be aware of before combat

✔ TRY ALL THE LEGENDS AND WORK OUT WHICH YOU PREFER

But remember, there's no advantage between them when it comes to speed, strength and combat ability.

✔ IF YOU CAN, PLAY WITH A DECENT SET OF HEADPHONES

You don't need a mic to play the game, as the Ping system takes much of the heavy lifting out of communicating. But, like all Battle Royale games, listening is key. You can get advance warning of trouble coming if you keep your ears open, and the sound is going to be clearer and more direct through headphones than through speakers. Unless you have exceptionally big and clear speakers and no other background noise!

✔ MANAGE YOUR INVENTORY

It won't matter early in the match, but as you accumulate loot, you're going to have to eventually pick what you need. You don't want to be fumbling in the midst of a firefight. Take time when you're away from the action and things are quieter, and quickly sort yourself out. Perhaps at the same time you should patch up your health and shields.

SHARE THE LOOT

There's little point being part of a squad if you hog all the good stuff to yourself. Yes, make sure you've got enough for your needs, but hand over any surplus loot to one of your squad mates. It's much easier to win if you work with each other.

GET ON TOP OF SWITCHING BETWEEN ITEMS

Make sure you know your Legend's abilities and which button does what. It's worth spending some time in the training level, as once you're in the match proper it can be pretty unforgiving!

RED BALLOONS ARE YOUR FRIEND

This is especially true if you need to get somewhere fast. Zipline to the top of them, then jump off. Your rocket pack will activate, then you can fly faster to where you need to be.

PLAY CAUTIOUS IN THE END-GAME

If you're down to the last three or four squads, that's the one time you don't want to start the battle. For a team to have survived that long, they have to be very lucky, very sneaky or excellent in combat. And if you're blasting away, you're instantly going to attract their attention. It's the hardest fight in the match.

Good luck, Legends. May the best – or luckiest! – squad win...

APEX LEGENDS: EXPERT TIPS

Don't shoot at the knockdown shield – punch it!

Knockdown shields are useful when defending yourself against oncoming enemies as they soak up bullet damage. Unfortunately, this can mean a waste of bullets, which is why we recommend punching the living daylights out of your enemy's knockdown shield instead. It's not as quick as shooting at the shield, but punching still does a solid 30 damage and saves you some precious ammo.

Read the numbers on the screen and know what they're telling you

The Apex Legends screen conveys lots of information, but there are some statistics you really need to keep an eye on. As well as always being aware of your own health and shields, remember that the colour of the damage counter when you land a hit gives you crucial data!

If you open your map/inventory while running, you'll continue to run

Sometimes you get caught in a bad situation and need to plan fast. For example, you've been ambushed by two different teams and you're sorely outnumbered, to the point where the only thing you can do is run. Pulling up your map whilst running leaves you plenty of time to Ping where you want your team to meet up, all without having to stop.

You can open your map whilst running

SLUM LAKES
ARTILLERY
THE PIT
RE
RUNOFF
CASCADES
WETLANDS
BUNKER
AIRBASE
BRIDGES
SWAMPS
HYDRO DAM
SKULL TOWN
MARKET
REPULSOR
THUNDERDOME
WATER TREATMENT

R1 SET WAYPOINT   L2 / R2 ZOOM   ◎ REMOVE WAYPOINT

MAP FEATUR
Respa
Bring ba
squad me

Supply
High tier lo

Hot Zone
High tier lo
for a fully kit

Supply Dro
Chance for hig

Pulling up your map whilst running leaves you time to Ping

Use open doors to climb higher and surprise enemies

The climbing mechanics are pretty good already, but what if we told you that opening a door, jumping up on it, then jumping on the nearest wall was possible? With this move, you're not only able to climb to higher, previously out of reach places, but also surprise enemies.

Downed teammates can block doors

You may think teammates are useless once they're downed, but you're very wrong. Depending on where they get downed, they can stop incoming enemies getting to you by placing their bodies behind the doors of buildings. This means the enemies must either kick in the door or go around another way to shoot at you.

Hanging onto walls or ledges allows you to peer over

You can hang onto ledges and climb walls

Give Lifeline the Ultimate Accelerant

Lifeline is all kinds of awesome. She can heal and revive you faster, and her ultimate ability calls in a Care Package that contains all kinds of rare goodies to help you succeed. Ultimate Accelerants restore 20% to your ultimate, which is hugely beneficial for Lifeline, as she has one of the slowest in the entire game.

Sometimes you just need to move

The characters may all move at the same pace, but sometimes it's worth packing away your weapon and making moving faster a top priority instead. Holstering a weapon and simply running can often be the best way out of a tough battle.

You can hang onto ledges to better observe

Jumping up walls is pretty darn cool. You can move faster and get over obstacles that can give you an advantage on the enemy team. However, hanging onto walls or ledges allows you to peer over and have a look at your surroundings without fully exposing yourself for the whole world to see. Unfortunately, you can't shoot from this position.

You can move death boxes, but not forever

When you kill someone in a firefight, your first reaction is to loot. However, this can lead to you being shot and killed. Instead, when you kill an enemy, move into their death box to push it forwards. Pushing it behind a rock or wall will allow you to loot it without the risk of getting shot in the head.

No fall damage means escape from tricky situations

Jumping from high places would mean certain death in some video games, but Apex Legends works differently. Getting away from an enemy team really is as simple as sliding off a cliff, allowing you to distance yourself without taking any damage in the process.

Wraith's teleport ability can get teammates out of the Ring faster

Depending on who you play with, some teammates can be running towards the next Ring the moment it's announced, while others will dilly dally until the Ring is just short of catching up to them. If you're playing Wraith, who can run a lot faster than characters like Pathfinder, Caustic and Gibraltar, you can use his ultimate to put up a portal, speed ahead, then drop it down again so your party can rush through. It isn't a perfect strategy, but it's very helpful when faced with slower teammates.

When you kill someone, wait before you loot

Pathfinder's grapple hook can be a deadly weapon

Green dots on the map indicate respawn points not used by your team

Checking your map can let you know where the nearest respawn points are – after all, they're difficult to miss with their huge icons. But did you know that smaller green dots indicate respawn points too? While you may be rushing to the nearest one, that isn't always the safest choice. Look for the next nearest green dot and head towards that instead.

Holster your weapon and move faster instead

Pathfinder's grapple hook can pull enemies towards you

Pathfinder's grapple is mostly used for getting around the map at high speeds, but it can also be used as a deadly weapon in the right hands. Catching an enemy unaware, you can pull them towards you, and get more than a few shots in whilst they scramble around helplessly.

Getting away from an enemy is as simple as sliding off a cliff

PUZZLE ANSWERS

PAGES 22-23

WORDSEARCH

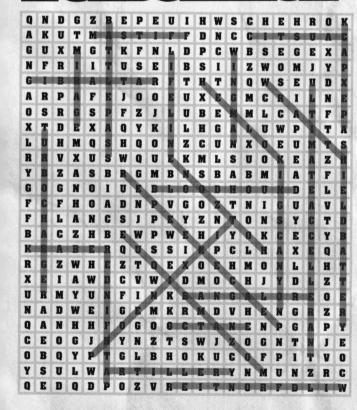

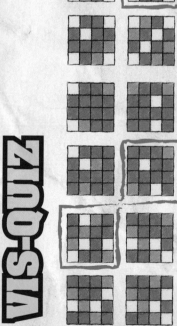

VIS-QUIZ

PAGES 54-55

VIS-QUIZ

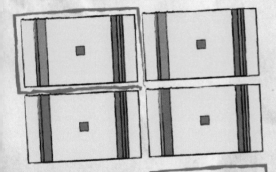

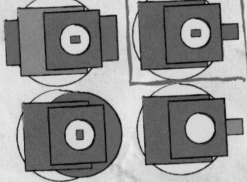

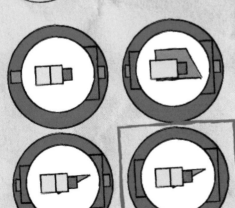

ANAGRAMS

Brag Alone
Bangalore

Blast Spate
Battle Pass

Tribal Rag
Gibraltar

Zen Hoot
Hot Zone

Conga Skinny
King's Canyon

Nil I Feel
Lifeline

Phat Friend
Pathfinder

Token Hip Xi
Phoenix Kit

Egor Carb Hunt
Turbocharger

World Niftier
Wild Frontier